FINDING COMFORT IN UNCERTAINTY

CHARLES "HOBS" HOBGOOD

authorHOUSE®

AuthorHouse™
1663 Liberty Drive
Bloomington, IN 47403
www.authorhouse.com
Phone: 1 (800) 839-8640

Published by AuthorHouse   04/29/2016

ISBN: 978-1-5246-0649-7 (sc)
ISBN: 978-1-5246-0648-0 (e)

Library of Congress Control Number: 2016906935

Print information available on the last page.

To Marabeth,

Whatever
my hand touches
is made better

by
your hands
touching mine

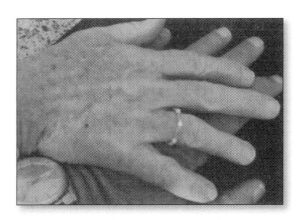

Author's Notes

The carousel of time brings us back to where old eyes see the world through a well journeyed heart. The old familiars are seen again as if for the first time. Each turn of the kaleidoscope brings larger visions. The necessary triumphs of youth no longer narrow our views of the world, unencumbered life becomes our gift to inhabit.

Little Cowboy

The youthful cowboy I once was still loves new trails. I ride a lot slower and have great difficulty mounting the horse. Yet, these days more is seen and taken into account which is what poets do.

It is my hope that these poems will enlarge the reader's world and bring comfort in uncertainty.

Therapist, Educator, Poet
Professor Emeritus Defiance College
Faculty American Youth Foundation-National Leadership Conference
Public and Private Mental Health Practice
Passion for Theology and Spiritual Journey
chobgood@defiance.edu

Take the Time

Take the time
to find comfort
in uncertainty

Time to live
into the mystery
To let the explosion of awe
give birth to ultimate concerns

Time to find
The deep-seated confidence
we call faith

Faith are human response
to what awe awakens
a harmony running through existence

To experience myself
As an intricate part of everything
To never stop asking questions
Questions that open doorways
Questions that make me human
Even among a billion stars

Stepping -Stone to Mystery

As a rabbit hops
out of his known
We too are limited by our familiar

Stepping- stones all around
Some clear, some disguised, some waiting
Some placed by invisible hands

Crossing streams that held us back
Stepping into far horizons
Over stones that bar our way

Some stones ancient and always
Some stones random and scattered
Some stones placed by necessity

Each stone a step into mystery
A ripening waiting to be tasted
Nurturing a deeper tomorrow

Out Beyond Convention

On Retreat, St. Benedict's Monastery
Snowmass, Colorado
Early spring sun filled day
a monk meditating
A solitary figure
In a snow- patched meadow
Gazing at snow covered peaks
Outlined by the Rockies bluest sky

His prayers edged into the hills
A pair of hawks glided
The monk's spirit and
the mountains spirit met
like the divine meets me.
All the non-sense I named truth
falls like leaves in autumn
And the views across the valley, well!

Nitty Gritty God

Nitty Gritty God
Shapes my mystical experiences
Beyond labyrinths, prayer beads,
bowed heads, bent knees.
An everyday God, everyplace God
Smiling through moon shadows
Winking from cereal boxes.
A God of surprise
Who never leaves us alone,
seldom fitting creeds or doctrine.
A God who is still speaking
Deep in each moment
Inviting us to alert presence.

Neither Logos nor Sophia

Icons without angels
a rudderless ship adrift at sea
Angels without icons
A tailless plane unable to land

Human Jesus without cosmic Jesus
a rocket without boosters
Cosmic Jesus without human Jesus
an airport without runways

The real work of the divine
Demands traffic between the realms
Human Jesus the access port
Cosmic Jesus grants full humanity

Feeding Frenzy

By the power of the sword
Heracles slay Hydra

The real battle is not_
will the shepherd protect
the lamb against the wolf?

The real battle is_
will the shepherds internal wolf
or lamb have the larger voice?
Depends?
Who will the shepherd feed?

Cousin to All

When your ripples in the pond of life
reach the far shores,
will they carry a message of hope?

Will you have lived in
a house of comfort?

Or will you have lived
Where the rains of justice fall
Where winds sing to rich and poor alike
Where prophets cry out against
indifference to suffering
Where "good people" sleep restlessly,
a holy haunting sewn into their fabric

I don't know about you.
For me prayer is a long loving look,
And when I pray my way through the day,
Seeing things through mindful eyes
I am compelled to act.

Breaking Open

If I open
every window in my house,
letting all the possible winds
blow through, will I blow away?

If I open
the door to my dining table,
inviting passers-by to eat
will I end up hungry?

If I turn
all my internal lights out
and sit in the dark with your light,
will my light be diminished?

If the king exchanges
his throne for an altar,
what will the kingdom look like?

As Blossoms Open and Close

Laying face up in bed
Picturing the night sky
like sleeping under the stars
A moment of surrender
ushers in a quiet miracle
wakefulness gives way to sleep

Despite our stubborn concerns
beyond the fears that chase us
in spite of clutter, dust, and worries
no matter how unfinished
a vastness soothes our soul

Without this innate meditation
like blossoms opening and closing
or a fly washing his face
There would be no beginnings
mornings breaking through darkness
rest giving birth to new dawns

Mystery

Wandering and Bumping

Leisure without contemplation
is idleness
Yet, thoughts will lead to doorways
which we choose is more complex

Falling into God
Undergoing God
That is what allows what happens
just to happen

And when we arrive
we say, "How did we really end up here?"
Back home again
without ever knowing it

Bumping and wandering
Doing our best
Doing what we hope is right
Open and trusting the next

Tucked In

All day long
rest easy
The canopy of night
sleeps under the sun

An endless blanket
vast beyond all comprehension
warms my humility
a tiny speck in the universe

Yet, billions of twinkling stars
shine as if just for me
Beauty a path through darkness
cradling me in wonder

A night sky meditation
billions of ancient candles glow
Breathe our regrets and sorrows
Breathe in a fresh new day

Thread Holders and Seekers

Each of us has a thread
Leading to a point beyond words
Where everything of this world
is drained to complete emptiness

In the place that seems void
We attach to absolutely everything
Where we begin and end, matters not, because
God's name is written in us.

Here beyond our will and works,
The divine has our personal map.
Hold tight and follow the thread.
Allow your life to emerge.

You are a seeker
Looking beyond conventional treasures
Guided by the blaze of God's light.
Awake to what is enough.

Swimming Lessons

Big fish and little fish
Swim easily in the Gulf Stream that
carries them on their journey

Do you think it is possible
we too swim in unseen streams?

Currents both subtle and strong
Subtle enough we don't notice
Strong enough they design our journey

Swimming alone and with everything
and if we ever once noticed

Our little self would no longer struggle
to proclaim our place
in the grandeur of it all

Son and Daughters of the High Desert

In the high desert
change has not obliterated
all that came before
faces of the earth are less altered
Here we seek elusive
color, shapes, textures, ancient footprints,
deeper peace, calling our own voice

Coming to this place of reflection
we may live slow enough
to muse and wonder
Experience the best and worst
of our ever -evolving selves
Moments become focal points
that appear to stop time
Hiking in timeless mountains
over gray rocks and black lava
up long dry streambeds
waiting for spring rains
life comes on its own terms

Invitation to a Cosmic Part

Exiled in the middle of time
Caught between birth and death
Busying ourselves not to fret
Yet, in those desert moments
Questions break through
So we build stories
Like toddlers circling
stuffed animals around their crib
We create rituals and symbols
to quiet our fears and
lift up our hopes
celebrate the possibilities
Rituals, symbols, stories
that attempt to explain
where is the home that protagonists
in every story are trying to find?
Where is our place
in the heart of mystery?

Somewhere between the bowels of the earth
and the furthest star
the teller of truth speaks,
"There is a binding element in the universe
and you are a non-replaceable speck
in the cosmic web wrapped in unbounded love."
So, I drum and sing
a great cosmic party
where we all dance with stardust!

Getting Dressed

God has slipped
inside your pocket
hanging in the closet

Getting dressed
you experience a little tug
can't sweet the small stuff

Nudges, tugs, bumps, twinges
tapings, nods, blind alleys, closed doors
can't pause your on a mission

God has slipped inside your pocket
so have your keys, billfold, pocket knife
small change, and a nail clipper

Ever wonder what slips by
when we're looking in front
or behind?
Check your pockets
has God slipped inside?

Detoxify and Drift

Muddled in the muck
I say, "I don't know."
The words wrap around me
like a thick wool blanket.
I step away from the warm fires
of knowing into cool uncertainty.
A fresh snow falls on the far hill.

Here the fringe folk sit with the holy.
Here rigid beliefs are not litmus tests.
Here seekers find inner authority.
Here mystics transcend constraints.
Here every element, "a word or book about God"
Here awake in the land of enchantment.

"A word or a book about God," by Mathew Fox

Myths that Deceive Us

Nothing is more difficult
than burying dead beliefs
What could be as easy
as blowing dandelion seeds
into summers tall grasses
becomes a weight too heavy to carry
when the seeds
accumulate myths of a lifetime

The ever- present wish for
simplicity and certitude
trumps flawed views
the only reality we have known
Imprinted on our minds
by a thousand voices
Crafted towers of mush
twisted to fit our agendas

For in burying dead beliefs
We enter a world we do not known
We watch a lifetime string of dominos
Tumble like falling leaves
And fight for what is wrong
Before seeing what terrifies us.

Silence

Trusting Silence

In that moment
of complete non-thinking
Where deeper knowing comes from
Call it intuition, call it contemplation, call it God
It is real and resides beyond will

A descending dove
Flies out of vast silence
A faithful act of trusting silence
Silence deep, spacious, wide
enough to hold contradiction and paradox

A trillion stars
with immeasurable space between them
from where mystery communicates
Those who learn to listen
become spacious and timeless

Stillness Thoughts

Stillness is the language of God
the rest is bad translation

Stillness has a home in nature
just after sunset the birds quiet

After a long night of waiting
in the morning the trees burst with song

You are more in stillness

In stillness you find
what you were when God formed you

And the stillness is the dancing

All translations of who God is
are betrayals

Holy books are the sharing of myths and prophets
insights from their deep communication with stillness

Abbott, "if the bishop does not feel welcome by my silence
he will never feel welcome by my words

Privilege or Not

Tell me I am old fashion
but I still feel ashamed at the sight
of what looks like unmerited misery

I avoid the words
"It is there fault"
"If only they would"
"This is the third generation"
How quickly we've built a world
that so easily blames the victim

How self- aggrandizing to claim
your accomplishments
To be blind to the glass stairway
of privilege leading to a magic door
that opens only by your thumb print
Congratulations on your legacy
admission to Yale, class of 2018

Old Familiar

Monastery bells at twilight
Wind chimes in a soft breeze
Salvation Army bells at Christmas

A cow moos
A puppy yips
A baby coos

Perhaps we make it all to complicated
Driven and striving

Penicillin is good
So too sitting on the front- porch swing!

Green Cathedral

After a long night
of waiting
In the morning the trees
burst with song

Just after sunset
the birds quiet
Welcoming you in stillness
to their sanctuary

An altar of leaves
whispers gentle song
Natures chorus
beacons you to listen

Stillness is the language
of God speaking still
Listen on the horizon
Evening's sky a blaze

Destination

Growing older
no longer lost
in pursuit of ribbons

A homecoming
to the neighborhood
where once I was enough

Spirit
no longer usurped
by outward journeys

The mastering of days
gives way to stillness
This moment becomes
everything I need

Desert Song

In the desert, stones teach _
Open your hand, drop the stone.
All the ideas you've cherished
Certainty blowing like tumbleweed,
Hum along with mystery's song
Sing like the wind through Palo Verdi
Pure and in harmony with silence

Back Side of Certainty

Out there someplace
there is a line
nature becomes a resource
people become voters
soldiers become body counts

A place where;
enchantment crosses into science
where the world we live in
becomes a world to own or control

A place where;
religion becomes creeds and doctrine
where the divine becomes the property
of the few and the right

And in that place;
we become alienated
from ourselves and each other
above and disconnected
from our brother earth
and our sister sky

And in that place;
moral justification
give birth to a blind child
and on and on until
no one remembers tears

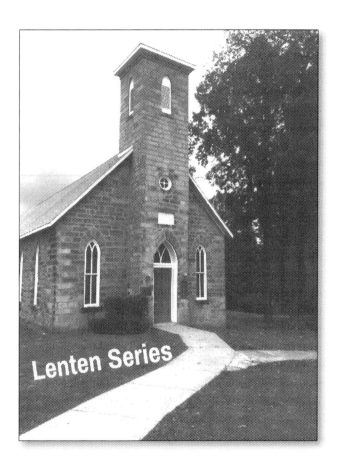

Lenten Series

A New Kind of Darkness

There at that moment of complete emptiness
Moments when emotions overwhelm us
When darkness breaks into our cocoon
Days like "Good Friday"
When cross- like events rain dark questions
Days prior to Easter hope
Days when our rationale minds
leave us alone and longing
for something beyond and more
Name it as you will, spirit, divine, God
And in that faith- filled moment of trusting darkness
Vast enough to hold ambiguity and mystery
These, "Good Friday" moments
Extinguish the light of the profane
Asking us to live through the darkness
and live into the light of mystery

Cross as Crossing Out the I

What if
Candles being extinguished mean
a new kind of darkness?
Not the darkness of the crucifixion,
rather extinguishing the lights
that lead our egos
Down paths of superficiality.

Paths where trinkets
glitter and glow,
millions of neon lights
turning the night sky
into day- blind stars.
What matters cannot be seen.
The sign above the monastery gate
reads, God Alone.

What if
each time we extinguish a candle,
we decide which bright shining distraction
we want to dim the lights on.
And as ego's lights begin to fade
shadows of infinite significance
loom on horizons.
Holy shadows beckon us
to simple make a cup of tea,
everyday events as sacraments.

Wind, Leaves, God, and Me

The wind swayed the leaves
The leaves rocking gently
Side to side, back and forth

The wind seems made for the leaves
The leaves made for the wind
How marvelous these moments

Yet, storms and darkness come and go
Leaves fall on cold autumn nights
Buds return after spring, s last frost

A wind as cool
as a mountain stream
A leaf warmed
by sun- bleached summer days

A leaf does not want
to be told about the wind
The leaf want to feel
and be touched by the wind

That's how it is
between God and me
How marvelous these moments
I seem made for God
and God seems make for me

Morning Walks

In the stillness of night's
ashen shadows
Just before morning's light
when the sun has yet
to warm the earth

Silhouettes of trees
join earth and sky
each stem faintly visible
A solitary bird cries into dawn
The sound echoes down the river

Here a quiet of descending
stairs leads to my inner self
A sacred space of serenity
where God's voice lives in me

Quiet morning walks
Awaken our deepest musings
Whispering loudly
to a sleeping world

Night Sky Meditation

All day long
rest easy
The canopy of night
sleeps under the sun.

An endless blanket
vast beyond all comprehension
Warms my humility
a tiny speck in the universe.

Yet, billions of twinkling stars
shine as if for me
Beauty a path through darkness
cradling me in wonder.

A night sky meditation
billions of ancient candles glow
Breathe out regrets and sorrows
Breathe in a fresh new dawn.

Palm Sunday

We are always in exodus
Looking for the Promise Land
Hoping to find a palm leaf trail
around each corner
Living with an invisible God
all the while holiness is calling
And when the sacred invites us to play
Oh my, Oh my!
Everything becomes precious.
Today's seemed terribly important
Does it really matter?
By next week the strawberries will be ripe and juicy

The day after Palm Sunday the streets are empty
Yet, Palm Trees grow in rich soil
Paths unfold where least expected
Promise Lands like rainbows
Beyond dreams, illusions, imaginings
Promise Lands become real
when seen through the heart's eyes

Awe & Wonder

Wash My Eyes

On my spiritual quest
I would stop darting and dancing
in every direction
Put aside my internal voice
Allow for just one moment
that I have nothing to say
And lay my silent empty head
in the lap of everything and nothing
I would ditch the trivial
one belief set no longer above another
I would take seriously
children starving in third worlds
I would wash my eyes clear
Use a soft cloth to rub away nonsense
I would gaze acrossed horizons
no longer clutter with my expectations
I would see that I am and
always have and will be part of everything

Unlocking Deeper Living

When you hold the sound of the ocean
deep in your ear
do you experience the life cycle of water
evaporation, condensation, precipitation
clouds circling the earth
A single drop of water blesses a solitary seed
then another until the entire planet is full

When you hold a stone in the palm of your hand
Do you experience the mountain it came from?
The enormity of time and pressure
shaping the majesty, building that shrine?

When you hold the warmth of the sun's
radiance against your skin,
do you experience the fire and energy
that pulses through all of life?
Blossoms peeking up from sun blanket earth
ebbing and flowing from dark to light.

Or do you live in a cultural trance?
Fleeting from moment to moment,
Thing to thing, desire to desire
Dancing with illusion, a tourist who only visits
Roots shallow and dry?

The sun, ocean, mountains each new day
invite you to unlock deeper living
Hold the moment tightly embraced like first
lovers on a star- filled night
Taking everything in, holding nothing

Under the Redwood Tree

A song touches you so much
you get to chocked to sing
A poem grabs you
pulls you to your knees
making the earth tremble
A story is so deep inside
if it does not come out
the pressure will break your bones

Here in a world full of noise
are syllables too fresh not to blossom
like wildflowers in a field of weeds
Living with the World Wide Web
the web crackles with lighting words
words full of static
words trying to replace everything before words

What does a thousand -year -old Redwood Tree say?
Take a vacation from words
sit silently under the Redwood Tree
How old do you need to be
before you can communicate
with a thousand- year -old tree?

This is not a Cheery Poem

If places and things never forget what they have witnessed
Then what does the lynching tree tell us?
If I spent the afternoon sitting in its shade,
what would I walk away with?
Is it possible to wonder through the woods and not have
spirit reach out?
Could I access these ancient wisdoms by climbing a
mountain peak?
Or do I cling to routines like the stability of the valley floor?
Fearful of being reminded of things I would rather forget
Yet what I long for and fear most is already inside me!
The wildest place in the lands inside of me
Terror and growth walk hand in hand
Between where I am and where I am going
Some will dare to step forward, while others hunker down
in the familiar?
In the end like everyone else we will greet the grotesque
There is a deep absurdity to existence!
Just asks me when I am dying of cancer in room 417
Do I wish I had greeted my brokenness before it is forced
upon me?

Sounds Familiar

In a world that hums
like a beehive
In a world so full of chatter
that it almost topples from noise
In a world where silence
haunts like death's ghosts
That world so full of busy
needs to give birth to a deep solitude

A solitude that forces you
back upon yourself
To a time before you were
To a time after you are
And forces you to ask
could that ever be?

Is eternity a stage of next
or has it always been?
Perhaps the real illusion
is the smallness of today?
And all my fears of non-existence
well, they can rest easy

And in the end as in the beginning
there will be a vast silence
That sound of our place
in the heart of mystery
It may not sound like
bees, mosquitoes, or mother's voice
But it will sound familiar;
it is the sound of home!

Parables of Wonder

Jesus told us parables
with no right answers
And we turned them
into simple one- liners
Seven loaves and fish becomes
a miracle that feeds hundreds
A rabbit pulled out of a hat
by the magician of magicians

The miracle is that people shared
The miracle is that something
more than fish can feed us
The miracle is that we too
can feed the hungry

Miracles happen
when we allow for mystery
under the scarf of uncertainty
It is not a slight of hand
but the letting go of the veil
of knowing we clutch for comfort

Look, the Field is Alive with Daisies

Trade wanting for enjoying
Wanting comes from fragmentation
as if something out there
will change something inside
Says, "we will be ok if only
we have the red dress"

Wanting always lets you down
never delivers what you hoped
promises diluted and broken
The mirror reflects you in the red dress
but you feel as before
needing even more to fill you out

Enjoyment comes from each moment
Linking you to the universe
Being alive with what is
Joy says, "Being right here
is just right for now"
Look, the field is alive with daisies

Living Well

You can't throw Jesus
out with the bath water
anymore than you can throw
the baby out the window
Yet, how do we resurrect
the historical Jesus?
Crucified by self- serving institutions
Double-teamed by the church and empire
creating a narrative Jesus
A message of fear and exclusion
original sin, redemption, and heaven

When this grounded Jewish mystic
offers us a model of living
through the divine that lives in us
A message of hope, love, and inclusion
"a way to live fully, love wastefully,
and be all that you can be"
Can we at least drain
the narrative waters
so that the living waters
rise to the surface
Becoming a mirror for our lives today?

Quote, "a way to live fully, love wastefully, and be all you can be"
From John Shelly Spong

Enough

Sit and watch enough sunrises
Sit and watch enough sunsets
You will see there is this moment
when ashen silhouettes of trees
lines the horizon
Neither coming or going
Neither being born or dying
Neither sunrise nor sunset
There in that moment
eternity opens before us
and if we can bask in that moment
letting enough wash over us
We become free from all fears
to live life as a gift given to us

Chance Encounter

Exchange blaming the darkness
for bring the light
Stoke the fires of light
by bringing your full attention

Even in chance encounters

Seek the indwelling light
deep in every living thing
The lamp will differ, yet the light unchanged
Fuels each lamp with your love

Announcement

Wisdom admonishes
Resurrection is beyond resuscitation
Rather, a wagering of your life
against the core conviction
Love is stronger than death
Spiritual identity formed
through self -surrender
survives the grave
never to be taken away
A journey through fear to love

Beginnings

Apron of Longing

The story of a raindrop
Is the story of amazement
The story of each soul
breathtaking and beholding

Resting in such heritage
Morning deserves new eyes
Only radical awe and wonder
greet such irresistible living

Dreams and visions
Processions beyond ordinary
Hold out an apron of longing
Gathering droplets of mystery

No longer seeking answers
Gates of surprise thrown open
Embracing the miracle of existence
Thank you our only prayer

The Bend in the Road

The bend in the road
Is a place
we go to and where
we've been before
and will go again

A place of sacred
groomed from familiarity
a personal retreat
a healing balm

A place we know
in winter, summer
fall, and spring
Watched the sun rise
Bleach, and fade

Where feet
meet solid ground
Where muscles taunt and tired
unknot, unwind, and relax
Where minds cluttered and confused
find solace in solitude

Omega Point

Where everyone belongs
Where everyone is co-creator
Where in everyone, every five years
70 billion cell are resurrected
Each cell with millions of even smaller particles

Everyone not only belongs
Everyone knows they belong
Everyone lives as if they belong
Who else would God be?
Where else would God be?

Hitching Post

Symbols
Remnants of experience
embrace us

Miles from the sea
shells on the windowsill
bring rhythmic ocean sounds

A song from your wedding
carries early dreams
regenerating emotions

Nana's large- print bible
stories that underpin
grounding our family

When we surround ourselves
with symbols of our truth
Like grandma's bowl of chocolate
we are filled with precious histories
Calling us to our better selves

Go Softly

When knowing softens
wisdom begins

When coldness softens
loves begins

When individualism softens
grace begins

When projection softens
surprise begins

When clinging softens
spirit begins

A Soul's Cage

A soul's cage
provides an oasis of safety
where our wings can not spread

When my beloved sings
music creases my fears
Safe to open the cage door
a yearning burst forth
to hold nothing back
The clash between
deepest yearnings and deepest fears
is softened moment by moment
by a mysterious alchemy of love
Two beloved's set each other free

Motley Pew

Dictionary Aside

The two greatest
English words are
Summer Afternoon

Served
in tall glasses
Of sweet mint tea

Under pastel
Yellow and green
beach umbrellas

Accompanied by
wordless songs
of rhythmic surf

Laughing Gulls glide
on currents of air
mirroring contentment

Time drifts easy
healing old bones
scared by harsher days

Worldly concerns
Disappear in
Sun-bleached sand

Long summer afternoons
Ready us
for life's winters

Hanging Out

Wall Street is no place
To learn the art of hanging out
Wall Street is crowded
with starched collars and heads congested
with cares and concerns
pockets bulging with dollars and Excedrin.

Chicago's Southside Senior Center
is a mecca for Hanging Out
African American men and women
Praise and rejoicing, the sounds of humanity
Born to oppression, journey through tribulation
The songs of the fields echo through old bones.
Singing and laughing they free the world.
Having freed themselves by forgiving life.
Desiring what they have, they have all things.
Clinging to each other and the lord.
They are just hanging out!

Within Mumbo-Jumbo Everything

Somewhere between
designer shoes and going barefoot
Between being part of a crowd
and being isolated
You and I can locate ourselves
Our childhood lessons
Like a horse wearing blinders
limiting our vision of other paths
And the blinder of blinders
are not around our eyes
but frozen in our minds

There is no time
For empire's conventional paths
For the pettiness of being annoyed
For the pursuit of self-importance
We need to keep our eyes
On the amazement of mystery
To live into that greater energy
which includes everything and us
which evolves always and forever
What to our western minds
appears to be mystical mumbo-jumbo
may just turn out to be what matters!

Wisdom's Way

Wisdom
is tethered
between realms
mediating the visible and invisible
How then shall we listen?
"He who has ears to hear
let him hear"
Not to the evening news
nor the latest NBA scores
The voice of silence
does not scream
"live from CNN's anchor desk"
Listen instead to the voice
of the decaying trees
on the floor of the forest
to the moss facing north

Inner Witnessing

You can't move
the plank
you're standing on
and if that plank
is the only self
you know
you will cling
for dear life

The fatal stew
is identifying
with your needs, agendas, and projections
They are the self
you are standing on

What would happen
if you didn't do
what you had hoped to do?
Stepping off the plank
of your regular ways

What really
would happen next?
Are dead agendas
like dead caterpillars
really butterflies?

If

No life without baggage
Trailing behind us like a bushy squirrel
First girlfriend dumped me
for the quarterback who beat me out
A zit glares at me from the bathroom mirror
looming larger than last night's pizza
My golf ball lands in high rough
three strokes later, championship lost
A thousand nit-shit details of woe
My tail anchors me in muddy waters

I stop to watch a squirrel
scampering on the electric line
His tail follows without anchoring
flipping right or left for balance
tossing over his head for shade

What would happen if _
I turned my baggage inside-out
sat my troubles down on the ground
stood on them to peer into new windows
If I, like the squirrel
Used my baggage as rudder
on a ship setting sail for new ports

Now, what really would happen if_
I stopped seeing all the nit-shit annoyances
as annoyances and saw them as tiny lampposts
on a trail of lifetime adventures
What really would happen?

Busy

Upon inquiry as to the conditions
of my friends
A universal answer
I am busy very busy

I am besieged by external demands
I am surrounded by lists of things to do

And if by some major act of God
the external demands were removed
and relegated to hell,

I'd then be assaulted by internal expectations
and mountains of should's
Streams flooded with shadowy hopes

Forgetting to look at the moon
Spending days never looking
into the faces of those I love.

These are not sins of omission
but signs of preoccupation,
And busy is the cancer
eating my life.

"God Created Man in His Image"

If God created man in his image
then God must look a lot like us
So the question becomes, does God wear designer jeans?
or maybe just tough rough Wranglers?
Imagine Wranglers endorsed by a Super Bowl quarterback
Bret Farve and God.
Imagine Bret and God just tossing the old pigskin.
Bret shows God his Super Bowl ring
God shows Bret the Grand Canyon
Bret asks God, if he would like a chili dog
God tells Bret he was incarnated as Christ,
A Jewish mystic and keeps kosher
Bret says," maybe you would like a beer?"
God says, "I am more of a wine guy"
It was my first miracle at the wedding,
and boy was I surprised by my mother asking
Bret says, "Are you, still making your own stuff"?
God says, "I could but I'd be happy
with a California Red, Paso Robles, 1991"

Grand love

Family Album

Gazing at the family album
Have you ever wondered
What was said or
What was thought
Just at that moment
Making them look that way?

Aunt Mazzie's eyes look glazed
Uncle Saul's eyes are fixated on the sky
Cousin lou is staring at the barn
Cousin Barb is glaring at Grandpa
Grandpa's eyes are deflected to the soiled ground
Grandma's eyes are closed as usual

Can't help but wonder
What stories those eyes
Want me to hear-
What are they saying?
I know
I need to hear.

Where Children Live

Children live with rumpled beds
Trampolines for leaping legs
Jumping with delight

Children live with clutter floors
Where Teddy Bears, Rabbits, Skunks
and Monkeys wait with love

Children run in yards where bushes
and trees, become windmills, ghosts,
forts, castles and penguins

Children keep treasure boxes
under their beds
with bottle caps, buttons, and shoestrings

Children watch butterflies
land on baseball caps
and feel welcomed

Children live where we all reside
but older folks
draw the shades

Tooth Fairy Resurrection

Science tells us
flowers blossoming in the spring
is not magic but
in the dead of winter
I long and wonder

When I was three
I put my baby tooth
under my pillow and snug blanket
In the morning the Tooth Fairy
exchanged it for a shiny quarter

Now older
I've killed the Tooth Fairy
Buried under mounds
of steadfast assumptions
clinging to a way I know

Believing at three
had an easy delight
like roasting marshmallows
fluffed and expanded
surprise unfolded everyday

By mid-life
I've accumulated
mounds of stuff and
even bigger piles of things
"I'm right about"

In my nursery I lived
free from expectations
Spied seagulls outside my window
hands all sticky from milkweed
dancing with Curious George

I need to resurrect the tooth fairy
believe good things are under my pillow
sleep outside the covers
say amen with gratitude
embrace the life that waits for me

Tooth Fairy Two

Granddaughter Lauren age seven
Three front teeth missing
Expected the tooth fairy to
exchange teeth for coins

Counting the change, I ask
"Why does the Tooth Fairy want the teeth?"
"Paw- Paw, "the teeth contain the memories
of the children"

How I love conversations
Where belief is suspended
Giggles and silliness take over
Lauren, can't believe, Paw -Paw, doesn't know

My mother passed away last fall
Seven pair of glasses in her vanity
What if they were all I needed
to see the world through her eyes.

What if half the stuff
I take to be true
were no more so than
baby teeth are just baby teeth

What if half the time
all these facts and knowledge
merely lead to my life being
dull, fuzzy, and grey?

What if there really is a Tooth Fairy?
What if you really can find good
merely by looking through the Tooth Fairies eyes.
What if magic and enchantment don't fade with age?

Journey Bravely

Woe to those
who lead little lives
who leave more inside
than ever gets used

Haunted by ghost
of unborn dreams
Looking toward tomorrows
that never come

Smothering their fires of hope
With wet blankets
If only they could ride their dragons
extinguishing fears from yesterday

In a world pestered by distortions
dreams are doorways for the brave
Courage comes and goes
hold on for the next supply

Imaginable

True love is transformative
Giving birth to union
Beyond and on a higher plane
A bridge between realms
Beyond flesh and blood
Where time and space no longer limit us
The object of our affection
becomes the subject of our truth
A change in consciousness

Solace, Musing, Mystery

Grandma is porch rocking
Not rushing to tell me her truths
Slowly rocking back and forth
Listening to the boards cracking beneath her chair
Watching for the first star to be born each night
Counting it a blessing to have hot soup
Covering her expectations with an orange-green afghan
Always replies, "Just Fine"
Hopes the goldfinch will return in the morning
Lives with the mystery of when the weather will turn
Nudging her feathered friends to head south
Mystery adds novelty to her life, nothing that needs solving

Something very comforting about just letting it be
Periods of reflection add clarity
Like knowing she moistens her toast with tea
Just like her Gram used to do, Gram did it for her dentures
She does it for her Gram
Funny odd ways of honoring, no need to-no need not to
She's solved the mystery of moistening her toast
She has not solved a lot of others
Something very comforting about letting it be

The mysteries of the universe cover her like a blanket of a thousand stars
like honey sweetening her nightly tea, no need to understand the chemistry
Know her Gram kept her honey in a porcelain jar
She does too, thinks it's the same jar
It's been a long while, can't be sure
Solace comes from musing and mystery
Could be a long winter
Could be her last.

When I am gone

I prefer a poet
to give my eulogy
Let the scientist keep me alive
as long as I can smell the flowers
but when the scent has gone
Remember me in bright colors
Outrageously gay music
The smell of the forest after a rain
Eat dark chocolates, lots of it
Then spread my ashes on the path
that leads into the mist and mystery
Pay the poet well
poets unlike sports figures
never do get there just do!

Printed in the United States
By Bookmasters